WILD~ FLOWERS

Wild Flowers

WILD~ FLOWERS

Fran Hill

A ROMANTIC HISTORY WITH A GUIDE TO CULTIVATION

[Fran Hill]

RUNNING PRESS

Philadelphia, Pennsylvania

Copyright © 1994 by Inklink

Concept, design, and editorial direction Simon Jennings.
Produced, edited, and designed at Inklink,
Greenwich, London, England.

Text by Fran Hill
Text edited by Diana Craig
Designed by Simon Jennings
Botanical illustrations by Julia Cobbold
Archive illustrations enhanced by Robin Harris
Title page photography by Neil Waving

Published in The United States of America
by Running Press, Philadelphia, Pennsylvania

Text setting and computer make-up by Inklink, London.
Image generation by T.D. Studios, London.
Printed in Hong Kong.

Canadian representatives: General Publishing Co., Ltd.,
30 Lesmill Road, Don Mills, Ontario M3B 2T6.

9 8 7 6 5 4 3 2 1
Digit on the right indicates the number of this printing.

Library of Congress Catalog Number 93-85516

ISBN 1-56138-194-2

This book may be ordered by mail from the publisher.
Please add $2.50 for postage and handling.
But try your bookstore first!
Running Press Book Publishers
125 South Twenty-Second Street
Philadelphia, Pennsylvania 19103-4399

WILD-FLOWERS

A ROMANTIC HISTORY
WITH A GUIDE TO CULTIVATION
ARRANGED IN THREE CHAPTERS

CONTENTS

INTRODUCTION
PAGE SEVEN

CHAPTER ONE
WILDFLOWERS IN HISTORY
PAGE NINE

CHAPTER TWO
WILDFLOWERS FOR GARDENS
PAGE TWENTY-FIVE

CHAPTER THREE
CARE AND CULTIVATION
PAGE FIFTY-THREE

BIBLIOGRAPHY & ACKNOWLEDGMENTS
PAGE SIXTY-FOUR

NATURE'S OWN SELF
*"I would devote a certain part of even a small garden
to Nature's own self, and the loveliness of weed life."*
JOHN D. SEDDING 1891

Introduction

Many North American and North European wildflowers have a common ancestry and include some of the loveliest of flowering plants, their hardiness allowing them to survive in extreme conditions. They can be both humble and at the same time exquisitely beautiful, with delicate flowers in subtle colors, often sweetly scented.

In this book, only a small number of wildflowers can be described, yet these show the wide range of color, form, and habitat these plants include. The emotive, medicinal, and economic importance of wildflowers to man, as well as their interdependence on insects and other organisms, are all powerful reasons for their conservation. With improved understanding of genetics and the technology of plant breeding, the potential of wildflowers for use as food crops, medicinal herbs, and attractive garden plants is enormous. This technology also has a vital role to play in the conservation of threatened wild species, and in preventing their extinction.

The creation of wildlife habitats in the garden and the propagation and planting of wildflowers are two ways in which we can all help to preserve our natural heritage.

"Saw the rainbow in the heaven,
In the eastern sky, the rainbow,
Whispered, 'What is that Nokomis?'
And the good Nokomis answered:
''Tis the heaven of flowers you see there;
All the wild-flowers of the forest,
All the lilies of the prairie,
When on earth they fade and perish,
Blossom in that heaven above us.'"

From "The Song of Hiawatha"
by Henry Wadsworth Longfellow (1807-82)

DEDICATED TO
OUR ENVIRONMENT
WHICH SUFFERS
IN SILENCE

CHAPTER

I

WILD-FLOWERS IN HISTORY

So will I build my altar in the field
And the blue sky my fretted dome will be,
And the sweet fragrance the wild flower yields
Shall be the incense I will yield to thee.
FROM "TO NATURE" BY SAMUEL TAYLOR COLERIDGE (1772-1834)

WILDFLOWERS IN HISTORY

FLOWERING PLANTS FIRST APPEARED ON earth between 136 and 195 million years ago. Until then, plant life had been confined to algae, ferns, cycads, and giant horsetails. From pollen analysis, it is thought that before the onset of the Great Ice Age, about 2 million years ago, there were about 500 species of flowering plants in existence, including many which still survive and flourish to this day.

The success of flowering plants has been due to the formation of seeds inside a protective capsule, resistant to adverse conditions such as drought and frost; within this protective coat, the seeds delay germination until conditions are favorable. (In non-flowering plants, the seeds and spores are exposed to the elements.) Flowering plants have also developed an interdependent partnership with insects: the plants supply the insects with a food source of pollen and nectar, while the insects aid pollination and the dispersal of seeds.

Other factors – soil type, temperature (affected by altitude and latitude), rainfall, wind, and sun – have a bearing on the spread of different plant families, too. Until the Great Ice Age, the climate in the northern hemisphere was mild, encouraging the growth of "tropical" vegetation. Then, dense sheets of ice began to move south from the Arctic, across North America and Northern Europe. As the glaciers advanced and the temperature dropped, plant (and animal) communities "retreated" to warmer conditions nearer the Equator. During the warmer interglacial periods, they tried to re-establish themselves in the north. The seed was carried back from the south by birds, insects, and the wind, to germinate wherever conditions were favorable.

In America, the ice sheet did not reach the warm southern states such as Alabama and Florida, so northern plants had a natural refuge from which to recolonize northern sites. In Europe, despite low sea levels creating limited land links with Britain, and between southern

Europe and North Africa, physical barriers such as the sea hindered the periodic north-south flow of plants. When the glaciers melted and sea levels rose, these land links were cut, and many plants were thus prevented from re-colonizing northern Europe. With the resulting permanent reduction in summer temperatures in the north, others were unable to re-establish themselves.

Further redistribution of wildflowers was carried out by man. As people migrated from Europe to the New World, they inadvertently carried the seeds of wildflowers mixed in with their crop seeds. Other plants, particularly those with medicinal and culinary properties, were deliberately introduced from southern Europe into Britain by the Romans, and from Britain into America by the Pilgrim Fathers and explorers such as Cooke. These plants escaped from cultivation to naturalize and establish themselves in the wild: fennel is just one example. (The movement seems to have been very much one way: the great American botanist Asa Gray (1810-1888) asked pertinently, and perhaps plaintively, why it was that so many European "weeds" (wildflowers) had become naturalized in America and so few American weeds in Europe.)

Flowering plants have become specialized in their structure and life-cycles to exist in many contrasting and sometimes inhospitable habitats, from the dry mountains and arid desert conditions of the south-western states of North America to the damp, fertile meadows and woodlands of north-west Europe. Some wildflowers that we still find growing today are survivors of the Ice Age, and include sea pink, buttercup, water lily, sedge, pansy, and poppy.

LANDING OF THE PILGRIMS.

11

A LEGACY OF FLOWERS

MANY WILDFLOWERS HAVE MANAGED TO SURVIVE in the wild for thousands of years, and mankind must ensure that it does not destroy this natural heritage. The demands we place on the environment are excessive, and this has resulted in the destruction of many wildlife habitats, with their associated plant and animal communities. The pressures we create include: pollution; intensive agricultural and silvicultural practices, and the excessive use of herbicides and pesticides; road- and house-building, and industrial development; and the mismanagement and destruction of woodlands and wetlands.

Concern for the loss of wildflowers from the countryside is not only of recent concern, however. The Industrial Revolution, that began in Britain in the latter half of the 18th century, threatened rural habitats, too, as the early 19th-century English poet John Clare sadly observed:

> *"Now this sweet vision of my boyish hours*
> *Free as spring clouds and wild as summer flowers,*
> *Is faded all."*

An awareness of conservation issues began to dawn – in the minds of some individuals, anyway. In the late 19th century, when the wild garden was a popular concept, a reader of the magazine "The Gardener" wrote in, describing how he had transplanted three cartloads each of daffodils and lilies of the valley to improve his garden woods. In reply, another correspondent, showing great foresight, protested against such unbridled plundering, pointing out: "There is something selfish in wholesale cartloading away of the flowers of our meadows, hedges, banks, and copses.... If encouraged it will endanger not the wild gardens but the woodlands."

Many wild plants are still under threat from the actions of individuals. The beautiful lady's slipper, for example, has been so persecuted by plant collectors and gardeners in Britain that it is now on the point of extinction. In many countries, it has had to be protected by law, and it is possible that other wildflowers and plants will need the same protection in the future.

On a broader scale, the collective action of farmers is having a devastating effect. The practices of using "clean" crop seed, selective spraying with herbicides, and burning of stubble are resulting in the disappearance of wildflowers, and in a landscape that is poorer for this loss. Many wildflowers once common on agricultural land are under threat, particularly annual cornfield "weeds" such as corncockle, poppy, cornflower, and pheasant's eye, which rely on cultivation or soil disturbance to bring them to the surface where they can germinate.

Papaver rhoeas (common poppy)
This wildflower has seeds that can remain fertile in the ground for many years, which is why it appeared on the battlefields in Flanders in Belgium – shells and bombs disturbed the ground, encouraging the seeds to germinate. As a result, the flower became a symbol of World War I.

Medicinal Uses

WILDFLOWERS HAVE BEEN USED for medicinal purposes since long before the time of the Ancient Egyptians. Papyrus records on the surgical uses of wild plants date back as far as 2980 BC. The Ancient Hindus used herbs to prolong life, and their knowledge of drugs and plant spices spread throughout Asia and eventually Europe. In Ancient China, it was believed that for every ill there was a corresponding natural remedy; at the end of the 16th century, the Chinese produced a compendium of nearly 2,000 medicinal substances of plant origin, many common in Europe, such as daisy, sweet flag, and plantain.

In Britain, herbalism existed long before the Romans invaded, bringing with them their own herbs and healing methods. The Druids, Celtic priests of ancient Britain, were skilled in the medical use of wild plants, and had seven sacred herbs: clover, henbane, mistletoe, monkshood, pasque flower, primrose, and vervain.

"HERE HOLY VERVAYNE AND HERE DILL 'GAINST WITCHCRAFT MUCH AVAILING."

In the early Middle Ages, the monks copied manuscripts and recorded the herbal uses of wild plants. They grew wildflowers and non-native herbs for medicinal and culinary uses, alongside their vegetable, salad, and fruit crops. Many herbals were later written, including *The Herball or Generall Historie of Plants* by John Gerard (1545-1612), *The Theatre of Plants* by John Parkinson (1567-1650), and *The English Physician* by Nicholas Culpeper (1616-54).

14

The seeds and roots of herbs and vegetables, and herbals such as Parkinson's and Gerard's, crossed the Atlantic in colonists' ships, returning ships bringing native North American plants back for cultivation in European botanic gardens. Several of these became naturalized and established themselves as wildflowers.

Many common wildflowers still in existence today have wide-ranging healing powers. A clue that they have medicinal properties can sometimes be seen in the name. "Wort," for example, means "medicinal plant," hence soapwort (*Saponaria officinalis*) – used for centuries as a soap replacement – and figwort (*Scrophularia nodosa*), used for sprains, swellings, and inflammations. Many drugs which were once extracted from plants are now manufactured synthetically. However, numerous common medicines are still based on plant extracts, and "wildflowers" are grown commercially as crops, for example, evening primrose, from which the oil is extracted.

In recent years, there has been a revival of interest in natural medication. This is a specialized subject, however, and self-administration of plant remedies can be extremely dangerous. Precise identification of species is difficult and potentially dangerous, and plants may also be contaminated with chemical sprays. For reasons of simple conservation, it is not recommended that plants are collected from the wild. Anyone wishing to use medicinal herbs should either grow them or buy them dried, and use them only to treat simple ailments, preferably under professional supervision.

Many wildflowers have also been used for cosmetic purposes: lovage to cleanse and deodorize the skin; vervain in bath preparations to treat skin disorders; the fruits of the wild strawberry to tone and whiten the skin, and combat wrinkles and freckles. The ground-up flower-tops of evening primrose were added to face masks, cornflower was used in bath preparations and hair tonics, and as an eyewash, while an infusion of fennel seeds with elderflowers and rose petals still makes an effective skin softener or, combined with honey and yogurt, smooths out wrinkles – perhaps leading to the old saying, "Fennel is for flattery."

WILDFLOWERS & FOLKLORE

MANY WILDFLOWERS have folklore and superstition attached to them, particularly associated with love, luck, and the weather.

Healing herb

St. John's wort (*Hypericum perforatum*) was believed to have infinite healing powers derived from St. John, and was regarded as protection against the devil. If hung above the door, it was thought to ward off thunder, lightning, fire, and witches.

Headaches & snake bites

Vervain (*Verbena officinalis*) has long been associated with magic and sorcery. Roman soldiers carried it with them for protection, and lovers used it in love potions. It was also believed to ward off the plague and, if worn around the head, to prevent headaches and snake bites.

Water of Life

The drops of dew and rainwater which collect in the center of the leaves of lady's mantle (*Alchemilla vulgaris*) were used by medieval alchemists, who believed them to have magical and medicinal powers.

Lucky clover

Clover (*Trifolium*) with four leaves is regarded as lucky, for, as an old saying goes:

*"One leaf for fame, one leaf for wealth,
One leaf for a faithful lover,
And one leaf to bring glorious health
All are in a four-leaf clover."*

16

Good luck

Chicory (*Cichorium intybus*) is said to bring good luck, especially for those on exploring trips. For this reason many of the early American settlers and, later, prospectors carried a root of the plant in their pockets.

Easing of the heart

Wild pansy (*Viola tricolor*) gets its name from the French *pensée* (a thought or remembrance), and is associated with love and "easing of the heart" – hence its other name, "heartsease." Superstition warns against picking pansies when the weather is particularly good because, according to the widespread old belief, this will soon cause rain.

Death omen

Violets (*Violaceae*) that bloomed in the fall were said to be a forewarning of death for the people on whose land they grew.

CICHORIUM INTYBUS (CHICORY)

VIOLA TRICOLOR (WILD PANSY)

A herbal love potion

*"Take elecampane (*Inula helenium*), the seeds and flowers, vervain (*Verbena officinalis*) and the berries of mistletoe (*Phoradendron serotinum*). Beat them, after being well dried in an oven, into a powder and give it to the party you design upon in a glass of wine and it will work wonderful effect to your advantage."*
FROM "A COUNTRY HERBAL"
BY LESLEY GORDON

VIOLACEAE (VIOLETS)

17

WILDFLOWERS IN COOKING

WILDFLOWERS ARE USED IN COOKING to add a decorative garnish or flavor to prepared foods and drinks, as salads or cooked vegetables, and for making teas, alcoholic drinks, preserves, and sweetmeats. For example, the uncooked leaves of brooklime, salad burnet, dandelion, wintercress, yarrow, wild strawberry, and lovage are tasty in salads, while the young leaves and shoots of borage and nettle cook well as green vegetables.

Leaves and seeds can also give added taste to food. Fennel seeds are used in pickles and marinades and for imparting an anise flavor to cakes. Corn-poppy seeds are sprinkled on bread and cakes and, mixed with honey, make a tasty dressing for fruit. The leaves of wild marjoram, wild thyme, and water mint are used fresh or dried as herbs for flavoring meat, in stuffings, and with vegetables. In praise of water mint, the herbalist John Gerard wrote: "The savour or smell of the water mint rejoiceth the heart of man."

The leaves of raspberry, blackberry, wild strawberry, and scented mayweed have long been infused to produce herbal teas, while rosehips, blackberries, dandelion and hawthorn flowers, and nettle leaves can be fermented into wines. In the 19th century, the poor reputedly drank foxglove tea as a cheap means of obtaining the pleasures of intoxication – but this is definitely not recommended, since foxgloves can be fatal!

Borage soup

Melt ¼ cup butter in a pan, add ½ cup short-grain rice and cook over a low heat for 2 minutes, stirring frequently. Add 3 cups vegetable stock and simmer for 15 minutes. Add ½ lb washed borage leaves and flowers stripped from their stalks, and simmer for 10 minutes. Season with salt and pepper, liquidize or press through a sieve, and allow to cool. Serve cold, garnished with whirls of double cream and borage flowers.

"I Borage give courage."

OLD PROVERB

18

Horseradish sauce

Horseradish root has a pungent, hot flavor. Grated and mixed with plain yogurt or cream, white wine vinegar, and a little sugar, it makes a delicious sauce for roast beef, smoked mackerel, or herring (the roots can also be applied to relieve chilblains!).

Wildflower sweetmeats

Marshmallow contains starch, albumen, sugar, oil, and gelatinous matter, and was used to make marshmallow sweetmeat. Other wildflower sweetmeats include crystallized stems of angelica and candied flowers of sweet violet, primrose, borage, and dog rose. These flowers can also be used to decorate salads and cold drinks.

Rose-petal jam

The flowers of dog rose have many culinary uses: rose-petal wine, rose brandy, rose vinegar, rose honey, and rose-petal jam. To make the jam, take 2 crammed cupfuls petals, and dissolve 2 cupfuls sugar in ½ cup water. Mix with 1 tablespoon orange juice and 1 tablespoon lemon juice, and add the rose petals. Simmer for half an hour, strain, allow to cool, then pour into a small glass jar, and cover.

Herbal coffee

The roots of dandelion and chicory may be used to make a coffee substitute. Dry the roots in the sun, roast in the oven until brittle, and grind coarsely.

ARMORACIA RUSTICANA (HORSERADISH)

ALTHAEA OFFICINALIS (MARSHMALLOW)

ROSA CANINA (DOG ROSE)

WILDFLOWERS IN ART

FOR THOUSANDS OF YEARS, wildflowers have been highly valued for their beauty, fragrance, and ability to arouse the emotions. They have been used as decoration, as religious symbols, and as popular subjects for art.

Throughout the Middle Ages, illuminated manuscripts illustrated with wildflowers and insects were produced on skin, vellum, parchment, and paper. Monks patiently decorated liturgical books and manuscripts with gilding and painting, using colors extracted from wild plants and mixed with egg and gum dissolved in water. The end of the 15th century saw some of the finest illuminated borders; many of these decorations were tiny, but the detail was so accurate that specific flowers can be identified.

In the early part of the 16th century, books and manuscripts concerning plants had begun to be printed and illustrated, using woodcuts to make reproduction more economic. With the invention of lithography in the late 18th century, medical botanical books with fine illustrations of medicinal herbs appeared, such as Woodville's (British) *Medical Botany* of 1790, and Bigelow's *American Medical Botany* of 1817.

Wildflowers can be seen in abundance in different forms of traditional needlework. Renaissance tapestries – known as "millefleurs" or "thousand flowers" – feature meadows scattered with a huge variety of flowers, sewn so finely that even leaf veins can be seen.

Wildflowers were a source of inspiration for several of the French Impressionist painters. The common poppy seems to have been a particular favorite, featuring in paintings by Van Gogh and Monet, for example.

In the late 19th century, the Arts and Craft Movement in Britain and North America concentrated on traditional materials and techniques in architecture, furniture, ceramics, textiles, printing, binding, jewelry, and silverware. William Morris, a leader of the movement, "borrowed" the colorful meadows of wildflowers from medieval tapestries for many of his designs. Everywhere, the twisting stems of plants with leaves and berries, briar roses, buttercups, and other common wildflowers could be seen, and these designs are still popular today.

SUFFRAGE TO ST. NICHOLAS
From the Margaret de Foix Book of Hours, France c.1470
NATIONAL ART LIBRARY, VICTORIA & ALBERT MUSEUM, LONDON
Among the many identifiable varieties of wildflower in this border, wild strawberries were symbolic of the fruits of righteousness in medieval times, and violets represented humility.

Wildflowers for Scent

As well as being used as perfume for the body, wild-flowers and herbs have always had a more down-to-earth role, too, in masking unpleasant odors. In medieval times, for example, wildflowers were scattered or strewed over the floor to impart scent and camouflage bad smells. In 1573, in his *Five Hundred Pointes of Good Husbandry*, Thomas Tusser included in his list of strewing herbs: marjoram, dog rose, tansy, violets, daisies, camomile, and germander speedwell. Other plants used were water mint, wild strawberry, sweet flag, ladies' bedstraw, maiden pink, and pineapple mayweed.

These scented plants were also dried and used as ingredients for cosmetics, scented pillows and cushions, fragrant sachets, and potpourris. Essential oils were extracted from these plants too, to make scented waters (the forerunner of *eau de Cologne* was a distillation of balm leaves made by monks in 17th-century Paris).

Meadowsweet (Filipendula ulmaria)
This was a favorite strewing herb in Tudor times, and according to Gerard's Herball, "The leaves and floures of meadowsweet farre excelle all other strewing herbs for to decke up houses, to strewe in chambers, halls and banquetting houses in the summer time, for the smell thereof makes the heart merrie and joyful and delighteth the senses."

22

Preserving & Displaying

MUCH PLEASURE CAN BE HAD FROM PRESERVING the beauty of wildflowers by drying and pressing them, and using them in many interesting crafts. Flowers for drying must be picked early on a dry morning after any dew has evaporated. Some need to be gathered after every bud has opened, and others early in development. Seed heads should usually be collected when fully ripe.

Plants must be dried in a warm, dark place with good ventilation, to prevent flowers from fading and mold forming. Strip the leaves off and gather the stems into bundles held with a rubber band which can be tightened as they shrink, and hang the bundles up so that air can circulate. Varieties particularly good for drying or for their seed heads include: chicory; columbine; dock; evening primrose; grasses and grains; Jacob's ladder; lady's mantle; mayweed; meadowsweet; mullein; poppy; St. John's wort; sneezewort; soapwort; sorrel; tansy; teasel; toadflax; vervain; wild carrot; and woundwort.

Fresh flowers and seed heads can also be preserved by pressing them immediately after picking. They should be placed carefully between several sheets of smooth blotting paper or tissue, and weighed down between heavy books or in a press. Leave to dry for a week.

Almost any plant can be pressed, but some plants retain their colors better than others. They can be used in many artistic ways – for example, in "habitat pictures" showing meadow, wood, or seashore scenes; in pictures based on a herbal or color theme; in flower samplers and greeting cards; or, sealed with polyurethane varnish, as decoration for candles or furniture.

"A weed is no more than a flower in disguise,
Which is seen through at once, if love give a man eyes."
SAMUEL TAYLOR COLERIDGE (1772-1834)

WILDFLOWERS & DYES

FABRICS SUCH AS LINEN AND COTTON can be dyed with natural plant colors for use in herb pillows, cushions, and scented sachets, and as the background to pressed plant pictures. These vegetable dyes were many of the original constituents of medieval paints. Green colors can be extracted from mullein, fleabane, lily of the valley, and nettle; greens and browns from comfrey, sorrel, yarrow, wild carrot, and weld; yellow and orange from St. John's wort, tansy, and toadflax; blues, purples, and pinks from blackberry, elderberry, and ladies' bedstraw; and blue from elecampane.

Making a vegetable dye

Vegetable dyes need a mordant or color fixative (this determines the color given up by the plant). Put 1½ teaspoons of bicarbonate of soda or salt into an enamel or steel pan three-quarters full of water. Add the fabric and boil for 1 hour. Leave to cool in the pan overnight. Empty pan and fill with fresh water until three-quarters full. Put dye plants into a nylon stocking, knot the end, and immerse in water. Bring to the boil and simmer for 1 hour to release the dye. Slowly immerse the fabric in the liquid and boil, stirring frequently, for 30-60 minutes, depending on the shade required. Remove the fabric, rinse several times, and hang out to dry.

The still room
In the Middle Ages, most houses and farms had a "still room" where wild-flowers with medicinal, culinary, and scent uses were hung to dry.

CHAPTER

II

F WILD~ LOWERS FOR GARDENS

WHEN DAISIES PIED AND VIOLETS BLUE
AND LADY-SMOCKS ALL SILVER-WHITE
AND CUCKOO-BUDS OF YELLOW HUE
DO PAINT THE MEADOWS WITH DELIGHT …
FROM "LOVE'S LABOUR'S LOST" BY WILLIAM SHAKESPEARE (1564-1616)

25

A Natural Partnership

WILDFLOWERS FIT INTO A COMPLEX WEB of interdependence with all other forms of wildlife, and with insects in particular. The earliest wildflowers are self-fertile, relying on wind or earliest known insects such as beetles to help transfer the pollen from the male anthers to the female stigma on the same plant; these flowers tend to be scentless.

Later, flowering plants evolved that relied for their survival on a more effective process: cross-pollination (the transfer of pollen from one plant to another of the same species). This ensured greater variety and success in producing "offspring." The work of cross-pollination depended on insects, however, so wild flowers developed two ways to attract these vital helpers – color and scent.

Flowers & scent

The scent in flowers is in the form of essential oils that are produced by the substance chlorophyll, in an inverse ratio to the amount of pigment or coloration in the petals. Thus, scarlet and orange flowers tend to be devoid of scent, while white flowers usually are the most fragrant. It would therefore appear that scent is a substitute for color. It is these essential oils which provide plants with their herbal characteristics.

Scent has various functions. The most evil-smelling plants tend to be poisonous – Nature's way of telling animals not to touch! Plants with an unpleasant scent (produced by essential oils similar to those in putrefying animal matter) tend to be pollinated by flies and midges.

Butterflies & moths

Pleasantly-scented flowers are visited by butterflies and moths, which are attracted by perfume, rather than by flower color. These insects are called "flowers of the air," for their beauty and their fragrance; many have their own scent, and may visit flowers with a similar perfume.

Flowers which open at night are usually white or yellow, and are pollinated by night-flying moths. The flowerheads remain closed all day to retain the scent, which is released later to attract the insects.

26

Attracting bees

The majority of wildflowers are visited by bees. Bees are blind to the color red, but are sensitive to the ultraviolet rays reflected from some red plants. They tend to visit blue or yellow flowers, which are often unscented. To guide them to the source of pollen or nectar, some flowers also have distinguishing marks or "honey guides"; these are often yellow, such as the rays of heartsease or the eyes of forget-me-nots. Others may be invisible to the human eye, but are revealed to bees by ultraviolet light.

Other wildflowers that attract by appearance are those with large and compound flowerheads or umbels such as wild carrot and cow parsley. They are visited mainly by flies and midges with short tongues, which are only able to gather nectar where it is produced in shallow cups.

Busy bees
Honeybees and bumblebees feed on nectar, which is sucked up through a proboscis that varies in length according to the species, and on pollen gathered in baskets or pollen sacs on the hind legs. The pollen sticks to the bee's furry coat as it goes from plant to plant in search of nectar. It "combs" the pollen from its coat with the first two pairs of legs, and transfers it into the baskets. The pollen and nectar supplies are taken back to the colony and used to feed adult or young bees, or to make honey.

Summer visitors
The Red Admiral and Painted Lady come from southern Europe and North Africa, and visit northern climes only in summer. Both species will lay their eggs on nettle, but neither can withstand cold winters and, unless they can find warmer conditions, will perish with the first frosts.

27

WILD ANCESTORS

THE MAJORITY OF GARDEN PLANTS are derived from wild species that have been introduced from other countries by plant collectors, and new varieties produced from them through hybridization (cross-breeding) and selection. For example, the garden pansies and violets of today have resulted from hybridization of heartsease (*Viola tricolor*) and other *Viola* species. Another example is Jacob's ladder, of which a more highly colored and compact form has been bred by crossing *Polemonium caeruleum* with *Polemonium reptans*.

Occasionally, a plant species will naturally form offspring dissimilar to the parent plant – a process called natural mutation. The new forms may differ in size, and in flower and leaf color and shape. If they are selected and propagated, new plant types are formed, known as cultivars or strains. Many garden plants have arisen this way from native wildflowers: the Shirley poppy, for example, is descended from the common poppy. The Reverend William Wilks of Shirley in Surrey, England, noticed one particular poppy plant that had flowers with a white edge. He collected the seed and, with careful breeding, eventually grew poppies in various colors.

With careful selection and breeding, colorful border annuals have been grown from the cornflower. Dwarf forms such as Polka Dot, with pink, red, purple, white, and the original blue flowers, and tall forms such as "Blue Diadem," are seen. Selective breeding for flower color and increased flower size does have its disadvantages, though, in that it can often lead to sterility and loss of scent and nectar, and value to insects.

28

Wildflowers for
Pond & Marsh

Many beautiful and colorful marginal and wetland plants can be grown on the pond edge, or in marshy ground. By planting wild rather than cultivated forms, insects such as bees and butterflies will be attracted.

Brooklime and water mint
Brooklime (Veronica becca-bunga), *and water mint* (Mentha aquatica) *are attractive to insects, and have a long-flowering summer season.*

Parnassia palustris (grass of Parnassus), *Veronica beccabunga* (brooklime), and *Mentha aquatica* (water mint) (see previous page), are all low-growing, spreading perennials that grow in wet soils or pond shallows, in sun and semi-shade. All produce flowers for a long period from mid- to late summer, and these plants are easily propagated from seed or by root division. Water mint is a very useful plant for making herbal baths and pillows.

Menyanthes trifoliata (bogbean or buckbean), *Iris pseudocorus* (yellow iris), and *Butomus umbellatus* (flowering rush) are hardy, spreading, aquatic perennials that grow in pond shallows or wet soils, in sun or semi-shade.

Bogbean, an old medicinal plant with fever-reducing properties, bears beautiful pink buds that open to white, fringed, star-like flowers, which bloom for a long period in spring and summer. Propagate by dividing the root in spring or fall, and planting in mud. Alternatively, sow seed in spring.

P. PALUSTRIS (GRASS OF PARNASSUS)

MENYANTHES TRIFOLIATA (BOGBEAN)

Iris pseudocorus (yellow iris)

Named after the Greek rainbow goddess, *Iris pseudocorus* (yellow iris) is a tall plant with smooth, sword-like leaves, and cheerful, yellow flowers in early summer. It is a good plant for honeybees and hoverflies, but it can be invasive and may need controlling. The flowers yield a yellow dye. Propagate by dividing the rhizome (fleshy root), or plant seeds in fall.

Butomus umbellatus (flowering rush) is a tall, handsome perennial with umbels of pink flowers carried on leafless stems in late summer. It has long, sword-like leaves arising from the base. Propagate as yellow iris.

Lythrum salicaria (purple loosestrife), a medicinal herb, was once used for skin complaints, dysentery, and internal hemorrhages. This handsome, tall perennial likes marshy ground, and looks good grown in large groups. In midsummer, it bears tall spires of reddish-purple, whorled flowers. Tolerant of semi-shade, it may be propagated by root division, cuttings, or seed sown in spring.

Butomus umbellatus (flowering rush)

L. salicaria (purple loosestrife)

31

GEUM RIVALE (WATER AVENS)

CALTHA PALUSTRIS (MARSH MARIGOLD)

Best used as dense ground cover, *Geum rivale* (water avens) is a low-growing perennial for the pond margin or damp woodland, in sun or shade. Beautiful flowers in subtle shades of pink, orange, and purple appear in early summer. Easily propagated from seed sown in spring or fall, it will hybridize with wood avens.

Caltha palustris (marsh marigold) has survived in the wild since before the last Ice Age. It has large, glossy, kidney-shaped leaves and masses of bright, sunny, yellow flowers borne on erect stems in spring. Propagate by rhizome division or by sowing seed in late summer.

Stachys palustris (marsh woundwort) is a hairy perennial with erect stems up to 3ft (1m) tall, that grows in moist and marshy places. Whorls of purple flowers, much loved by bees, are produced in mid- to late summer. Sow seed in moist compost in spring or fall, or directly into soil in fall.

Other suitable pond and marsh plants are: *Acorus calamus* (sweet flag), *Alisma plantago-aquatica* (water plantain), *Althea palustris* (marshmallow), *Juncus effusus* (soft rush), *Luzula pilosa* (hairy woodrush), *Myosotis scorpioides* (water forget-me-not), *Myriophyllum spicatum* (spiked water milfoil), *Nasturtium officinale* (watercress), *Nuphar spp.* (yellow water lily), *Ranunculus aquatilis* (water crowfoot), and *Ranunculus flammula* (lesser spearwort).

STACHYS PALUSTRIS (MARSH WOUNDWORT)

WILDFLOWERS FOR
SEMI-SHADE & DAMP SHADE

A WIDE VARIETY OF WILDFLOWERS thrive in damp, shady conditions, or in dappled light on, say, the edge of a woodland. In the garden, they will grow in a damp shrubbery or mixed border, or under trees.

Wild strawberry
(Fragaria vesca) *is a low-growing, hardy perennial that makes a good ground-cover plant, spreading by runners. Small, delicious fruits follow dainty, white flowers in early summer. The bright green, hairy leaves give off a musky scent as they die in the fall. Propagate by planting runners. Wild strawberry will also grow in sun, and has various culinary uses.*

AQUILEGIA VULGARIS (COLUMBINE)

AJUGA REPTANS (BUGLE)

SEMI- & DAMP SHADE

Aquilegia vulgaris (columbine) is a hardy perennial growing to 2ft (60cms), and will thrive in sun or partial shade. Dainty, intense, blue-purple, drooping flowers, that are attractive to bees, appear in early summer. All parts of the plant are poisonous. It is easy to propagate, either by root division or by planting seed in late spring or early summer.

Ajuga reptans (bugle), a very useful, low-growing, ground-covering perennial, spreads naturally by runners. It flowers all summer, producing blooms that are normally blue-purple, but may be pink or pale blue. It will also grow in sun, but needs moist soil. Propagate either by division or by taking cuttings.

Ranunculus ficaria (lesser celandine) is a low-growing perennial with glossy, dark-green foliage and cheerful, bright-yellow flowers that appear in early spring. It thrives in semi-shade and damp shady places, and will also grow in sun, in grass, or culti-vated soil, but it can be invasive. Propagate from seed sown in spring, summer, or fall, or by splitting and replanting the tuberous roots.

RANUNCULUS FICARIA (LESSER CELANDINE)

Geranium robertianum (herb robert), a medicinal herb used in previous centuries to ease digestion, is a low-growing annual that will thrive in rocky areas and in sun, as well as in shade. It has dainty foliage and tiny, pink flowers from late spring to fall, and looks good with taller plants such as columbine growing through its foliage. It readily seeds itself.

Vinca minor (lesser periwinkle), a good ground-cover plant, has trailing, rooting stems, and shorter, erect stems carrying blue, purple, or mauve flowers in early summer. An evergreen, it thrives in ordinary garden soil, in shade or sun. Increase by dividing old plants, or by taking cuttings.

Angelica sylvestris (wild angelica) is a tall, statuesque, perennial herb with large clusters of greenish-white flowers in early summer. It will also grow in damp meadows, and on pond margins. Its flowers look attractive dried and, as indicated by its other name – "Holy Ghost plant" – it was once used as a safeguard against poison, hydrophobia, plague, malaria, and enchantment. Angelica self-seeds profusely, but dried seed may be sown in the fall.

GERANIUM ROBERTIANUM (HERB ROBERT)

VINCA MINOR (LESSER PERIWINKLE)

ANGELICA SYLVESTRIS (WILD ANGELICA)

SEMI- & DAMP SHADE

Silene dioica (RED CAMPION)

Oxalis acetosella (WOOD SORREL)

Glechoma hederacea (GROUND IVY)

Silene dioica (red campion) is a perennial woodland plant with attractive, pinkish-red flowers in midsummer. It will also grow in sunny meadows. It may be easily grown from seed, and will hybridize with white campion to produce pink campion.

Oxalis acetosella (wood sorrel), a delicate, woodland plant, thrives in shade or semi-shade, and spreads well in fertile soil. The pretty, light leaves curve downwards at night and in cold weather, while the white flowers – which appear in spring – close in dull or cold weather. Wood sorrel may be propagated from seed.

Glechoma hederacea (ground ivy), an old medicinal and culinary herb once used in making ale, is an evergreen, low-growing, ground-covering perennial. Small, mauve, lavender-like flowers are borne in early spring. It will grow in either sun or shade, but prefers a rich, moist soil. Ground ivy is easily propagated from seed sown in spring or fall.

Other plants to consider for semi-shade and damp shade are: *Geum urbanum* (wood avens), *Impatiens capensis* (spotted or orange touch-me-not), *Myosotis sylvatica* (wood forget-me-not), *Polygonatum multiflorum* (Solomon's seal), *Rosa canina* (dog rose), *Rubus fructicosus* (blackberry), *Rubus idaeus* (raspberry), *Symphytum vulgare* (comfrey), *Veronica chamaedrys* (germander speedwell), *Viburnum opulis* (guelder rose), and *Viola* species (violet).

WILDFLOWERS FOR ROCK, SCREE, & DRYSTONE WALLS

WILDFLOWER SPECIES GROWING wild on rock and scree (loose rock and stone at the base of a cliff) are specially adapted to survive windswept conditions, and tend to be low-growing. Many will grow in dry, grassy areas, or in rock gardens or gravel.

Wild thyme
(Thymus serphyllum*) flowers throughout the summer. The Romans planted it near their beehives for its flavoring qualities. A hardy perennial, it grows in sun and semi-shade, in most conditions.

PULSATILLA VULGARIS (PASQUE FLOWER)

ROCK, SCREE, & DRYSTONE WALLS

A perennial now rare in the wild, *Pulsatilla vulgaris* (pasque flower) is a useful medicinal herb and dye plant. It prefers an alkaline soil in full sun, but will also grow in semi-shade, or in dry grassland. It has attractive, feathery leaves, and produces silky buds that open to rich-purple flowers in spring. Propagate pasque flower by sowing freshly gathered seed in midsummer.

A low, carpeting perennial, *Armeria maritima* (thrift) bears dense heads of pretty, star-shaped, rose-pink, or white flowers that are especially attractive to butter-flies. For best effect, plant together in bold groups. Thrift prefers full sun, and will tolerate wet or dry conditions. Propagation is by seed in spring, or by cuttings.

ARMERIA MARITIMA (THRIFT)

An excellent culinary herb with an onion-like flavor, *Allium schoenoprasum* (chives) is a perennial that, in midsummer, bears rounded heads of pinkish-purple flowers, at the top of leafless stems. With its tufts of rush-like leaves, it looks best planted in bold groups, and also makes a good subject for window boxes or pots in full sun. It readily self-seeds, but can also be propagated by division of small bulbs.

ALLIUM SCHOENOPRASUM (CHIVES)

As an old medicinal herb, *Potentilla anserina* (silverweed) was used for its astringent and anti-inflammatory properties. A low-growing, spreading perennial, it forms good ground cover. It has silky, downy leaves and bears yellow, buttercup-like flowers on long stalks throughout summer. Silverweed can be propagated from runners or seed.

Dianthus deltoides (maiden pink) is an attractive, low-growing, perennial plant with narrow, grey-green leaves and single, rose-red flowers that bloom all summer. It prefers an acid soil, and self-seeds readily.

POTENTILLA ANSERINA (SILVERWEED)

DIANTHUS DELTOIDES (MAIDEN PINK)

SOLIDAGO VIRGAUREA (GOLDEN ROD)

ROCK, SCREE, & DRYSTONE WALLS

Solidago virgaurea (golden rod) was used in former times as a medicinal herb to treat internal and external wounds. A perennial plant, it grows in sun or semi-shade, and spreads to form clumps. Spikes of small, golden-yellow flowerlets bloom from midsummer to fall. Golden rod also makes an attractive addition to the flower border. Propagate by root division, or by sowing seed in spring or fall.

S. OPPOSITOFOLIA (PURPLE SAXIFRAGE)

TANACETUM PARTHENIUM (FEVERFEW)

Try also *Saxifraga oppositofolia* (purple saxifrage), *Tanacetum parthenium* (feverfew), and *Polemonium caeruleum* (Jacob's ladder) in these conditions.

POLEM. CAERULEUM (JACOB'S LADDER)

40

WILDFLOWERS FOR SUNNY, MOIST MEADOWS

MANY LOVELY MEADOW WILDFLOWERS were once a common part of the countryside but, with changes in farming practices, many are now restricted to damp, waste places or roadside verges. In the garden, they will grow in any moist, open site.

Ragged robin
(Lychnis flos-cuculi)
With its lovely, ragged, rose-red blooms, flowers all summer. Ragged robin is an attractive perennial that grows in most moist soils in sun or semi-shade, and is best in bold drifts. Sow seed into moist compost in spring or summer.

41

CARDAMINE PRATENSIS (CUCKOO FLOWER)

SUNNY, MOIST MEADOWS

Cardamine pratensis (cuckoo flower or lady's smock) is a small perennial that bears pretty flowers of pale lilac or pink, veined with darker violet, in early spring. It will grow in sun or semi-shade in most moist, fertile soils. It readily self-seeds, but may also be propagated from seed in summer or early fall.

An old medicinal herb used for poultices and in cough syrups, *Malva moschata* (musk mallow) is a bushy perennial with large, rose-pink, or occasionally white, flowers and bright-green, dissected leaves that give off a faint musky smell if run through the hand in warm weather. Musk mallow flowers all summer, and is popular with bees. It will grow in sun or semi-shade, and is easily propagated from seed.

MALVA MOSCHATA (MUSK MALLOW)

42

Once used as a cure for chest problems – and to ward off lightning – *Chrysanthemum leucanthemum* (ox-eye daisy, moon daisy, or marguerite) is an attractive, erect, woody perennial that will grow in most soils in sun or semi-shade. Sunny-yellow and white flowerheads are produced all summer, and are much liked by insects. Ox-eye daisy looks best planted in bold drifts with grasses and other meadow plants, and is easily propagated from seed sown in spring or fall.

C. LEUCANTHEMUM (OX-EYE DAISY)

Ranunculus acris (meadow buttercup) is a common, yet beautiful, meadow perennial. Low-growing with pretty dissected leaves, it produces cheerful, yellow, rose-like flowers, borne at the end of flowering stems, in midsummer. It prefers sun but will also grow in semi-shade. To propagate, sow seed in spring or fall, mixed with the seeds of other meadow wildflowers and grasses.

R. ACRIS (MEADOW BUTTERCUP)

A once-common meadow plant similar in appearance to dandelion, *Leontodon hispidus* (rough hawkbit) produces bright-yellow flowers all summer, and will grow in most soils, including chalk. As a medicinal herb, it was used to treat jaundice and liver complaints. Propagate rough hawkbit from seed sown in spring or fall.

LEONTODON HISPIDUS (ROUGH HAWKBIT)

43

G. PRATENSE (MEADOW CRANESBILL)

C. NIGRA (COMMON KNAPWEED)

SUNNY, MOIST MEADOWS

Geranium pratense (meadow cranesbill) is a striking, many-stemmed perennial with large, mauve-blue flowers all summer. In the wild – where it has suffered from more intense agricultural work – it reaches 2ft (60cm), but will grow much taller in fertile soil. It thrives in sun or semi-shade, and is easily grown from seed in spring or summer.

An old medicinal herb used to treat wounds and bruises, *Centauria nigra* (common knap-weed or hardheads) is a very useful, perennial wildflower that grows in most fertile soils and sit-uations in sun or semi-shade. A good bee and butterfly nectar plant, it produces purple-reddish, thistle-like flowers from mid- to late summer that look attractive in dried-flower arrangements. The flowerheads may be used to extract yellow-green dye. Propagate from seed in spring.

Pulicaria dysentaria (fleabane) is an old medicinal herb used for dysentery and skin disorders. Its name derives from its use as an insecticide: it was burnt to drive out fleas and lice. A perennial for wet meadows or pond margins, it has a creeping rootstock, erect, woody stems reaching 2ft (60cm), and furry, crinkly leaves. Cheerful yellow blooms are produced in late summer. Propagate by root division in fall, or seed sown in fall or spring.

PULICARIA DYSENTARIA (FLEABANE)

44

Wildflowers for Dry, Sunny Grassland

A WIDE RANGE OF BEAUTIFULLY COLORED and often delicate wildflowers will grow in dry, sunny conditions. Several of these provide important nectar supplies for insects, or breeding sites for butterflies. In the garden, they will grow in any well-drained site in full sun.

Harebell
(Campanula rotundifolia) *is a delicately beautiful perennial that bears dainty, blue, nodding flower heads on slender stems in late summer. Harebell will grow in sun and semi-shade in most soils, and may be propagated from seed in spring.*

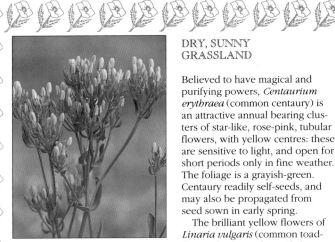

C. ERYTHRAEA (COMMON CENTAURY)

LINARIA VULGARIS (COMMON TOADFLAX)

DRY, SUNNY GRASSLAND

Believed to have magical and purifying powers, *Centaurium erythraea* (common centaury) is an attractive annual bearing clusters of star-like, rose-pink, tubular flowers, with yellow centres: these are sensitive to light, and open for short periods only in fine weather. The foliage is a grayish-green. Centaury readily self-seeds, and may also be propagated from seed sown in early spring.

The brilliant yellow flowers of *Linaria vulgaris* (common toadflax or "bacon-and-eggs"), borne profusely in late summer and fall, are a magnet for bees. With its small, waxy leaves, this creeping perennial can be invasive and may need controlling: to check self-seeding, cut off flowerheads before the seeds ripen. Propagate from seed in spring and fall.

An important butterfly-breeding plant, also visited by bees, *Lotus corniculatus* (bird's-foot trefoil) is a low-growing, carpeting perennial. Yellow and crimson buds open to bright-yellow flowers, tinged with orange and brown, in early summer. Bird's-foot trefoil thrives in most dry soils, and amongst rocks, and may be propagated from seed in spring or late summer.

LOTUS CORNICULATUS (BIRD'S-FOOT TREFOIL)

46

The funnel-shaped, red or dull-purple flowers of *Cyanoglossum officinale* (houndstongue) bloom all summer and provide an important source of nectar for bees and butterflies. Also useful as a traditional medicinal herb, this tall, erect biennial has long, downy leaves, and thrives in sandy or chalky soil. Houndstongue self-seeds easily; it may also be propagated from seed in late summer, but needs a hard winter frost to germinate.

Anthyllis vulneraria (kidney vetch or ladies' fingers) is another useful plant, both as a medicinal herb with soothing and astringent properties, as an important food source for bees and as a breeding site for butterflies. A low-growing perennial, it has silky, pale-green leaves, and large, rounded heads of downy, nectar-rich flowers throughout summer. It favors a well-drained soil. Kidney vetch can be propagated from seed in spring or early fall.

Knautia arvensis (field scabious or blue buttons) was once used for treating leprosy. It is a large plant, and its prolific, mauve, pin-cushion flowerheads, that appear in late summer, attract bees and butterflies. Although it prefers a chalky soil, it will tolerate most fertile, well-drained soils. Seed is difficult to germinate. Sow in spring or fall, and lightly cover with compost.

C. OFFICINALE (HOUNDSTONGUE)

ANTHYLLIS VULNERARIA (KIDNEY VETCH)

KNAUTIA ARVENSIS (FIELD SCABIOUS)

47

GALIUM VERUM (LADIES' BEDSTRAW)

SANGUISORBA MINOR (SALAD BURNET)

V. CHAMAEDRYS (GERMANDER SPEEDWELL)

DRY, SUNNY GRASSLAND

Galium verum (ladies' bedstraw) is a dye plant and old medicinal herb used to stop bleeding, and as a laxative. In the 16th century, it was used as cheese rennet, to curdle milk. A low-growing perennial reaching a height of 16in (40cm), it thrives in well-drained soil, in sun or semi-shade, spreading by underground runners. It produces whorls of narrow leaves and clusters of small, bright-yellow flowers on erect stems in midsummer. Since it can be slow to germinate, sow seed in fall.

Sanguisorba minor (salad burnet) is a culinary herb with a taste of cucumber, used in salads and as a seasoning. An attractive perennial, it bears toothed, evergreen foliage and dark, reddish-green, pompom flowerheads all summer. It favors chalky soil and readily self-seeds, and may also be grown from seed sown in spring or fall.

Veronica chamaedrys (germander speedwell) is a striking, creeping, or taller-growing perennial reaching a height of 14in (35cm). Dainty, bright-blue flowers with a central eye are borne in spring and early summer. Germander speedwell grows in most soils, in short or long grass, and in sun or semi-shade. Propagate by splitting plants.

48

Wildflowers for the Cultivated Border

THE FOLLOWING SUGGESTED BORDER PLANTS are weeds occurring naturally in either cultivated or waste ground, that will grow well in most fertile soils. Most of the other wildflowers described elsewhere in the book can also be grown in the border.

Viper's bugloss

Echium vulgare (viper's bugloss) *is a beautifully colored, tall-growing biennial, used as a medicinal and culinary herb. Funnel-shaped flowers, turning from rose to blue or white, are borne profusely all summer, and are much loved by bees. Viper's bugloss likes a sunny position, and prefers alkaline soil, although it will tolerate slightly acid conditions. It self-seeds freely.*

Anagallis arvensis (scarlet pimpernel) is known as "the poor man's weatherglass" – wide-open flowers mean fine weather, closed flowers warn of rain. This delicate, low-growing, sprawling, annual plant will grow in good, cultivated soil in full sun. Bright red, starry flowers are borne all summer. The plant readily self-seeds.

Tanacetum vulgare (tansy) is a tall, perennial plant, with medicinal and culinary uses. It has finely divided, feathery leaves, and flat clusters of yellow flowers appearing in late summer. It prefers a sunny position. It self-seeds easily, and can be propagated by root division in spring or fall.

TANACETUM VULGARE (TANSY)

CULTIVATED BORDER

Digitalis purpurea (foxglove) is an attractive biennial for sun and shade. Loved by bees and insects, it has large, ovate, downy leaves and tall stems bearing many purple, pink, or white, bell-shaped flowers in early summer. The plant is highly poisonous, but has been used to treat scurvy and heart complaints. Heart drugs are now extracted from it. Foxglove self-seeds readily, and is also easily grown from seed.

DIGITALIS PURPUREA (FOXGLOVE)

Dipsacus fullonum (teasel) has been in existence since the last Ice Age. This tall, prickly biennial, with its "architectural" quality, produces spiky, conical, lilac flowerheads once used to tease the nap on cloth – hence its name. The flowers are loved by bees and, when dried, stay on the stems all winter, providing seed for birds. Teasel is also useful as a dried-flower plant. It is easily grown from seed sown in spring or fall.

DIPSACUS FULLONUM (TEASEL)

An old medicinal herb used for respiratory and gastric disorders, *Malva sylvestris* (common mallow) is a tall, bushy perennial with large, ivy-shaped leaves and showy, rose-purple flowers all summer. The fresh leaves on young shoots can be cooked as a vegetable. Mallow is easily propagated from seed in spring or fall.

MALVA SYLVESTRIS (COMMON MALLOW)

CULTIVATED BORDER

Once believed to have the power to drive away evil spirits, *Verbascum thapsis* (mullein) is a tall, erect, biennial plant, able to reach a height of 6ft (1.8m), and clothed with soft, whitish, woolly hairs. Single spikes bearing clusters of single flowers rise from a rosette of woolly leaves, and bloom all summer. It prefers a chalky, well-drained soil in a sunny, windless position. Propagate from seed in spring.

Oenothera biennis (evening primrose) is a biennial plant with large, thin-petalled, delicately-scented, yellow flowers which open at dusk from summer to fall. The oil is extracted commercially for medical uses. The root can be boiled as a vegetable. Tolerant of most soils in sun or semi-shade, it is easily propagated from seed in spring or fall, or by dividing roots or offsets. It self-seeds readily.

An old medicinal and dye herb, *Daucus carota* (wild carrot) is a hardy biennial or short-lived perennial of medium height. It grows in sun and most soils, and is also suitable for the wildflower meadow and rock garden. It has divided, carrot-like leaves, and beautiful, flat, white flowerheads that bloom all summer. Its seed-heads look decorative when dried. It readily self-seeds, and may also be propagated from seed sown in spring or fall.

VERBASCUM THAPSIS (MULLEIN)

O. BIENNIS (EVENING PRIMROSE)

DAUCUS CAROTA (WILD CARROT)

CHAPTER

III

CARE AND CULTIVATION

When skies are gentle,
Breezes bland,
When loam that's warm within the hand
Falls friable between the tines
Sow hollyhocks and columbines …

VITA SACKVILLE-WEST (1892-1962), FROM "THE ILLUSTRATED GARDEN BOOK"

Growing Wildflowers

Most of the plants referred to in this book can be easily grown from seed but, if you are growing shrubs and perennials, this is a slow process, and other propagation techniques can be used. No wild plant should ever be dug up from the countryside – there is no reason to do so, since many nurseries supply wildflowers and herbs in pots ready for planting.

Sowing from seed

The cheapest way to grow wildflowers is from seed. This can be bought from merchants, several of whom trade by mail. Seed can also be collected from common, locally abundant wildflowers, but care must be taken not to take too much, or to damage or trample surrounding plants.

If you already have established wildflowers in the garden, there should be a plentiful supply of seed to collect. Most seeds should be gathered when the fruit or seedheads are brown or black, dry, or dry and fluffy. Some are best gathered before fully dry, and a paper bag lightly tied over a ripening seedhead will catch seed as it falls.

Wildflower seed is generally best sown in the fall in trays of compost, covered with a sprinkling of compost, protected with a sheet of plastic or glass, and left to over-winter out of full sun. The cold temperature is often a prerequisite to germination. Wetland-plant seed and seedlings need to be kept permanently moist. Methods of pricking out and potting on are as for garden plants.

Root division

Many perennials can be physically split in two by dividing the roots and leaves. Others will grow from pieces of root or, if they have a rhizome (a type of swollen, fleshy root), this can be divided into pieces, each having an "eye" or bud. Each piece should then be replanted. Divide in winter or early spring.

Growing from offsets

Bulbs and corms produce offsets, or small bulbils on the outside of the parent bulb. These can be carefully broken off, and planted out.

Taking cuttings

Many perennial wildflowers can be propagated from soft-wood cuttings. Cut the ends off young stems about 2in (5cm) long, and carefully remove the lower few leaves. Dip the cut ends into root-promoting hormone powder, and insert into a pot or tray filled with light, sandy compost. Water gently, cover with a plastic bag to keep moist, and place in a warm, light position, out of direct sunlight.

Once the cuttings have rooted, plant into pots filled with non-peat potting compost. Keep young plants shaded and moist. Gradually move them into cooler temperatures before planting out into their final positions in the garden.

Growing from runners

Plants such as wild strawberry send out overground stolons or shoots, known as runners, which produce roots at intervals along their length. Where these roots make contact with the soil, they take hold and grow to produce new plants. These can then be detached from the parent plant by severing the runners, and planted out in spring or fall.

Natural self-seeders
Many wildflowers, particularly annuals such as the long-headed-poppy shown here, produce copious amounts of seeds, which readily germinate around the plant, or are carried to other sites by birds, to germinate later.

"The poppy is painted glass; it never glows so brightly as when the sun shines through it... always it is a flame, and it warms the winds like a blown ruby."

JOHN RUSKIN (1819-1900)

55

The Organic Garden

WILDFLOWERS MAY BE GROWN for their color and charm alone but, with careful planning, the garden can also become a refuge or haven for a host of beautiful insects and mini-beasts. Just watching their fascinating activities can add a whole new dimension to gardening, even if all you have is the smallest of backyards. By creating a healthy garden environment with a variety of habitats to attract other forms of wildlife, the gardener can play an important role in conservation – in many respects creating a miniature nature reserve on the doorstep. To achieve this kind of wildlife garden, it is best to adopt organic gardening techniques that avoid or minimize the use of chemical fertilizers, pesticides, and herbicides.

Soil care

Organic material should be used to make potting and seed compost, and to improve soil structure and fertility. Although they are of organic origin, the use of peat-based

Attracting bees and butterflies
Grow Symphytum officinale (common comfrey) *in a sunny spot, and its pretty, white, pink or purple bell-shaped flowers will bloom all summer and draw masses of bees and butterflies.*

composts is ecologically unacceptable, and the many alternatives available should be used: coir, spent hops, well-rotted manure, treated sewage, and – the cheapest and best – garden compost made from rotted, non-woody, garden and kitchen waste that can be recycled back into the soil.

Wild plants themselves can also be used to make natural fertilizers. Comfrey, for example, is rich in potassium, and nettle in iron, and both are good sources of nitrogen. If leaves are steeped in water (about 1lb/450g in 10pt/6 litres water) for 4–5 weeks, the resulting solution can be used as a liquid fertilizer and foliar feed.

Natural pest control

Several wildflowers can be grown to make organic substitutes for chemical pesticides. Aphids and other pests, for example, can be sprayed with an infusion of elder leaves and chives, or tansy, wild thyme, and feverfew.

Another useful practice is known as "companion planting," in which certain wildflowers are planted next to cultivated plants and food crops – which by selective breeding have become highly susceptible to disease – to help ward off pests. Many members of the daisy family, for example, such as fleabane, tansy, elecampane, and feverfew, have pest-repellent properties and, if these are grown amongst crops, they appear to strengthen their neighbors, and encourage resistance to pests and disease, and generally increase the health of the garden. Camomile, yarrow, foxglove, and borage have a similar effect on pests.

A healthy wildflower garden, however, should also attract natural predators to keep pests under control. For example, toads, ground beetles, small mammals, and birds will eat snails and slugs (so don't put down poison); ladybirds will feast on aphids; and predatory hoverflies, wasps, and dragonflies will control other insect pests.

Flowery Lawns & Borders

MANY OF OUR ONCE-COMMON WILDFLOWERS and agricultural weeds, such as poppies, can be conserved by planting flower-rich lawns and borders in the garden (using border and meadow plants from Chapter II).

Creating a flowery lawn

Many gardens will have insufficient space for the kind of flowery hay meadow in which wildflowers once grew; it is possible, though, to grow a variety of meadow species in only a few square yards of land, if a new mowing regime is adopted.

To create a true meadow, it is first necessary to reduce the soil fertility to prevent strong-growing grasses from swamping wildflowers. In order to do this, strip off the turf with a few inches of soil, and dig over the earth, removing any thistle or dock roots. Till finely with a rake, and sow a grass-seed and wildflower-meadow seed mix suited to the soil type, or plant pot-grown wildflowers. This should be done in fall or spring, in dry weather. After sowing, level the soil lightly, and water the seed in with a fine spray.

To maintain a meadow with spring- and early-summer flowers, any cutting should be delayed until midsummer; for late-flowering plants, delay cutting until the fall. To ensure the spread of plants, flowers must be left to go to seed. Cut the meadow with a hand scythe or wheeled, rotary mower with the blade set fairly high. Leave the cuttings to dry, occasionally turning them to let the seeds drop, and rake off.

Another easy and attractive idea is to plant wild, spring-flowering bulbs in the fall. These will give a colorful display early in the year, and the leaves can be mown off once they have died back.

Creating a flower border

A beautiful flower border can be created by growing wildflowers and shrubs alongside garden varieties chosen for their food value to insects and birds. Wildflowers tend to be more subtle than their ornamental counterparts, with their larger, sometimes brash flowers, and will be shown to greatest effect if grown in bold drifts or groups. Unlike ornamental flowers, too, that often clash if colors from the opposite sides of the spectrum are sited together, wildflowers seem to grow quite happily side by side in opposing colors.

Grow both early- and late-flowering varieties to provide nectar for the longest time possible – for early bees and butterflies emerging from hibernation, and for insects preparing for hibernation in late summer. Site the border in a sunny position to attract insects, and avoid the use of chemical fertilizers, pesticides, and herbicides. Hand-weed, composting all non-woody plant material. Flowers can be deadheaded before they set seed, to help prolong the flowering period, but you should eventually allow seedheads to ripen to provide an important food supply for birds and small mammals (as well as for your own dried-flower arrangements).

Colorful country scene
A riot of color can be provided by arable "weeds" such as blue cornflower, pink corncockle, red poppy, scarlet pimpernel, yellow corn marigold and buttercup, and white ox-eye daisy. Seed should be sown into well-drained but fertile soil in a sunny position. Including barley, oats, or wheat will create an evocative scene.

Ponds & Pond Margins

WETLAND WILDFLOWERS are suffering considerably from the loss of their natural, freshwater habitat. Creating a pond and marshy area in your garden will be a positive step towards conserving  some of our loveliest wildflowers, and the host of invertebrates and amphibians that depend on that habitat.

Pond style & site

The best way to build a "natural" pond is to line a hole with a flexible butyl liner. Pre-formed fiberglass liners look unnatural, and steep sides do not create the right conditions for marginal wetland plants, or for animals crawling in and out of the water.

Site the pond in an open, sunny position, away from overhanging trees. The best shape, whatever the size of pond, is like that of a saucer, with gently sloping sides down to a center depth of 32–36in (80–90 cm), or more, if possible. (If the pond is very small, the depth may be shallower.) This depth will ensure that, in the severest of winters, aquatic animals will be able to escape any ice that has formed in the surface layers of the pond.

Constructing the pond

Begin by digging a hole to the required shape, but 8in (20cm) deeper than the required, finished depth, to allow for the liner, soil, and sand. Retain the topsoil.

Smooth the hollow, removing any sharp stones, and firm the surface well. To ensure protection for the liner, line the hollow with a 1in (25mm) layer of sand, and overlay with polyester matting.

Lay the liner in the hollow, taking care not to puncture it. Do not pull it taut or trim the edges yet. Spread a second layer of matting over the liner, and cover it with a layer of topsoil, 5–6in (12.5–15cm) deep. Trim the edge of the liner, ensuring enough is left to tuck under the surrounding turf or paving, depending on which edging treatment you have chosen. Fill the pond slowly, trickling the water onto a piece of plastic to prevent the soil from being dislodged and exposing the liner.

Edging the pond

To create different planting conditions, build a rock garden next to the pond, perhaps allowing it to slope down to a gravel beach along one side of the pond. Provide miniature "caves" in the rocks for frogs and newts, and flat-topped rocks for "sunbathing" animals. Along another section, continue meadow planting right up to the pond edge. An area of paving (with gaps between pavers for creeping plants) somewhere along the pond margin will provide a useful, firm foothold for carrying out pond maintenance, or for observing pond life.

Planting the pond

Try to plant as many native pond plants as possible, to provide feeding and breeding conditions for aquatic animals. Remember that it is essential to include oxygenating plants.

Pond maintainance

To maintain a healthy pond, some water plants will need to be split, and excessive growth of oxygenating plants and algae controlled. Dead vegetation and debris must also be removed, to prevent decay and water stagnation. To help keep the water clear, wedge a bale of barley straw,from a farm or pet shop, into the pond: although it is not fully understood how this works, the straw seems to inhibit the growth of algae.

Pond visitors

Once filled and planted up, the pond will soon be colonized by insects, frogs, toads, and newts, as well as a host of bottom- and surface-dwelling invertebrates, which will arrive naturally, on pond plants or the feet of visiting birds. Among pond visitors, the most beautiful and spectacular will be drag-onflies and damselflies.

Rocks, Paving, & Containers

Wildflowers readily colonize old, neglected walls and paving, and even rooftiles, germinating in dirt accumulated in crevices. In fact, many wildflowers, such as those which grow on rocks, scree, and sea cliffs, have adapted to survive in such conditions. Colonizing plants are not always confined to low-growing species: even the tall foxglove and valerian will self-seed into odd places.

Planting in walls & paving

In the garden, paving and walls can be designed to provide a foothold for plants. Paving can be dry-laid on sand and rubble, or spot-bedded with mortar. Leave gaps between the paving which can be filled with soil and seeded with creeping, scented plants, such as wild thyme or scented mayweed. Both creeping species and tall, architectural plants may be grown in gravel. If it has a bound (well-rolled and firm) finish, a hole can be created and filled with soil. The gravel will form a mulch around the roots, and conserve moisture.

Creating a rock garden

Many beautiful wildflowers favor an alkaline soil. If you live in an area of acidic soil, you could build a limestone or chalk rockery bank in which to grow alkaline-loving plants, provided that collected rainwater is used for watering. When constructing a rock garden, work on the principle that rocks tend to look more natural if weathered, if two-thirds of their bulk is buried in soil, and if they are laid with their naturally weathered sides showing. Use soil and gravel of similar pH (acidity or alkalinity) for the planting pockets and mulching. For the chalk bank, put a thick layer of limey soil over a mound of chalk or limestone rock.

Containers

Most wildflowers can be grown in containers of all shapes and sizes. Wood, stone, or clay containers usually look more pleasing and appropriate for wildflowers than their plastic counterparts. They should have sufficient drainage holes, and be clean and free from disease and

Mini-meadows

A single species of bright wildflower, such as poppy or cornflower, in one container can look stunning. Mixing wildflowers and garden plants gives a pleasing effect. In a large enough container, such as a window box or stone trough, even a mini-wildflower meadow or cornfield can be grown.

pests, before being filled with a layer of broken rocks to aid drainage, and a proprietary, standard-strength, soil-based potting compost, or homemade compost/soil mix. Plants should be fed at least every 4–5 weeks during the growing season, ideally with an organic fertilizer.

Vertical planting

House walls can provide vertical growing space, and wild climbing plants such as honeysuckle, old man's beard, ivy, and dog rose, can be grown alongside garden varieties that have nectar- or berry-value to insects and birds. Timber or mesh trellis panels should be fixed to walls or fences on batons, to hold the plants slightly away from the wall. Plants can be grown in large containers and, once established on the trellis, will provide hibernation sites for butterflies (between the trellis and the wall), nesting sites for birds, and a food source for wildlife.

*"There grew pied wind-flowers and violets,
Daisies, those pearled Arcturi of the earth,
The constellated flower that never sets."*
FROM "THE QUESTION"
BY PERCY BYSSHE SHELLEY (1792-1822)

BIBLIOGRAPHY

Many books and journals have been consulted,
and the following will be found to make useful and pleasurable reading:

Herbs R. Phillips, N. Foy, Pan Books, 1977
Pocket Guide to the Wildflowers of North America
P. Forey, Dragon's World, 1990
Systematic Guide to Flowering Plants of the World
S. A. Manning, London Museum Press, 1965
The Wildflowers of Britain and Northern Europe
R. Fitter, A. Fitter, M. Blamey, William Collins, 1974
Wildflowers of the United States (12 vols)
H. W. Ricket, McGraw Hill, New York, 1966-76
Wildlife Gardening, a Practical Handbook
F. Hill, Derbyshire Wildlife Trust, 1988

USEFUL ADDRESSES

The Center for Plant Conservation,
125 Arborways, Jamaica Plain, Massachusetts 02130
The Herb Society of America,
9019 Kirtland-Chardon Road, Mentor, Ohio 44060
The National Wildflower Research Center,
200 FM 973 N, Austin, Texas 78725
English Nature,
Northminster House, Peterborough, PE1 1UA, UK
The Herb Society,
P.O. Box 415, London SW1P 2HE, UK

ACKNOWLEDGMENTS

The producers gratefully acknowledge the following individuals,
organizations, and sources that have assisted in the
creation of this book.

FOR THE SUPPLY OF PHOTOGRAPHS :
Harry McMahon and other members of
the Derbyshire Wildlife Trust
FOR THE CREATION OF ORIGINAL ILLUSTRATIONS:
Julia Cobbold
FOR THE COLORING & ENHANCEMENT OF ARCHIVE ILLUSTRATIONS:
Robin Harris
FOR PICTORIAL REFERENCES &VISUAL MATERIAL:
The Natural History of Plants
Kerner & Oliver, The Gresham Publishing Co., 1904
The History of The United States
Alexander H. Stephens, Hickman & Fowler, 1882
The Dover Pictorial Archive series
"Suffrage to St. Nicholas"
from the *Margaret de Foix Book of Hours*
National Art Library, Victoria & Albert Museum